WIMBLEDON TO BECKENHAM
BEFORE TRAMLINK

John C. Gillham

MP Middleton Press

Cover pictures:

Front upper - Class D1 0-4-2T no. B615 calls at Beddington Lane just prior to the commencement of electrically operated services (H.F.Wheeller/R.S.Carpenter)

Front lower - Unit no. 5793 rumbles over the points at the east end of Mitcham Junction station as it works the 14.30 from West Croydon to Wimbledon on 26th March 1973. (J.Scrace)

Back - The exterior of Woodside station was smart and clean when photographed in August 1992. (J.Scrace)

Published February 2001

ISBN 1 901706 58 3

© Middleton Press, 2001

Design Deborah Esher

Published by
    Middleton Press
    Easebourne Lane
    Midhurst, West Sussex
    GU29 9AZ
Tel: 01730 813169
Fax: 01730 812601

Printed & bound by Biddles Ltd,
    Guildford and Kings Lynn

CONTENTS

ACKNOWLEDGEMENTS

All the photographs in this book that are not credited were taken by the author in the last two weeks before the closure of the Wimbledon to West Croydon and Addiscombe to Elmers End railways unless otherwise dated. I am very grateful to the photographers noted in the caption credits for having the forethought to take the others. My gratitude is recorded for the assistance given by John B. Gent on Central Croydon matters. I must also thank Godfrey Croughton and Norman Langridge for providing the tickets.

Additional relevant photos and information can be found in several other Middleton Press books, notably *Croydon to East Grinstead* nos 1-8, *Lines around Wimbledon* nos 24-32, *Mitcham Junction Lines* nos 47-54 and 77-120, *London Bridge to Addiscombe* nos 66-75 and 96-119, *West Croydon to Epsom* nos 1-19 and *Clapham Junction to Beckenham Junction* nos 103-120.

The provisional Tramlink diagram was published in
1991 in this form. Only a few names of stops were changed subsequently.

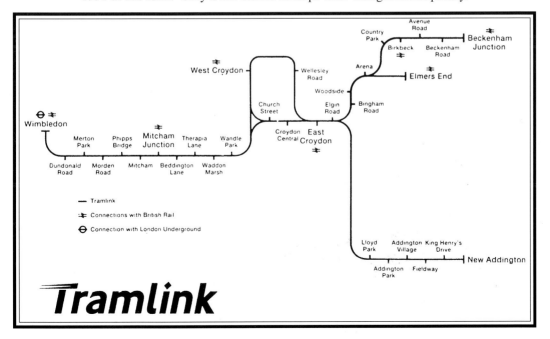

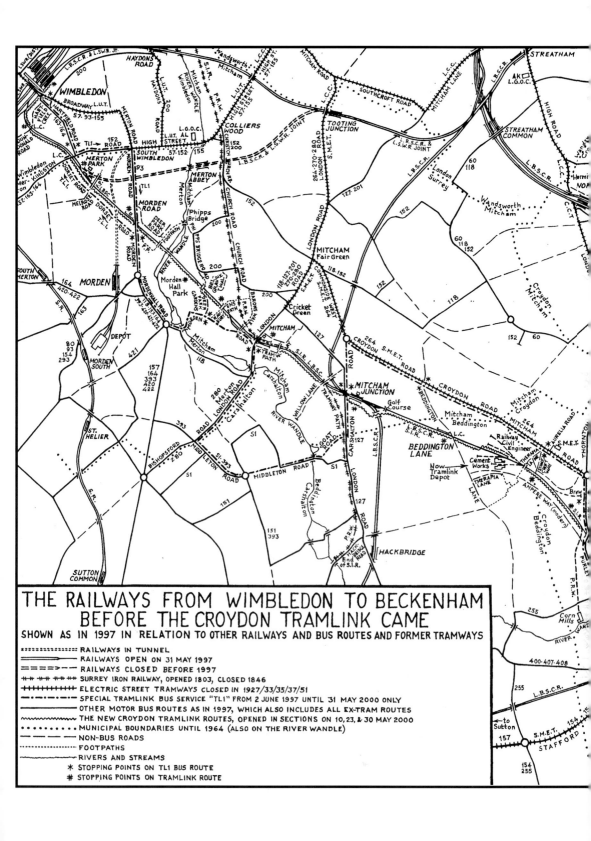

THE RAILWAYS FROM WIMBLEDON TO BECKENHAM
BEFORE THE CROYDON TRAMLINK CAME
SHOWN AS IN 1997 IN RELATION TO OTHER RAILWAYS AND BUS ROUTES AND FORMER TRAMWAYS

- RAILWAYS IN TUNNEL
- RAILWAYS OPEN ON 31 MAY 1997
- RAILWAYS CLOSED BEFORE 1997
- SURREY IRON RAILWAY, OPENED 1803, CLOSED 1846
- ELECTRIC STREET TRAMWAYS CLOSED IN 1927/33/35/37/51
- SPECIAL TRAMLINK BUS SERVICE "TL1" FROM 2 JUNE 1997 UNTIL 31 MAY 2000 ONLY
- OTHER MOTOR BUS ROUTES AS IN 1997, WHICH ALSO INCLUDES ALL EX-TRAM ROUTES
- THE NEW CROYDON TRAMLINK ROUTES, OPENED IN SECTIONS ON 10, 23, & 30 MAY 2000
- MUNICIPAL BOUNDARIES UNTIL 1964 (ALSO ON THE RIVER WANDLE)
- NON-BUS ROADS
- FOOTPATHS
- RIVERS AND STREAMS
- ∗ STOPPING POINTS ON TL1 BUS ROUTE
- # STOPPING POINTS ON TRAMLINK ROUTE

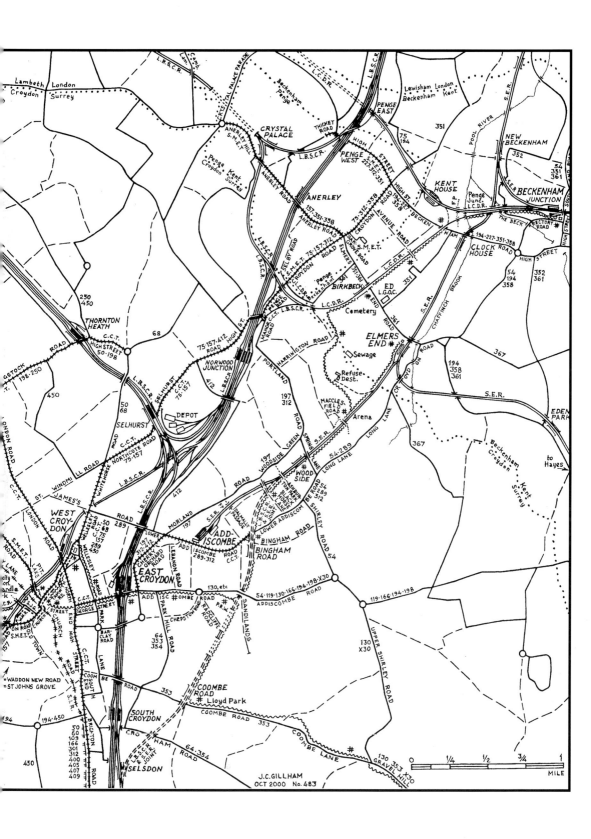

J.C. GILLHAM
OCT 2000 No. 483

GEOGRAPHICAL SETTING

Wimbledon, Croydon and Beckenham are respectively seven, ten and nine miles south from the centre of London, and are on fairly level and low-lying ground. Three to four miles south of Croydon a range of hills (the North Downs) rises to more than 700 feet, but the main road and main railway from London to the south coast via Croydon pass due south through a gap in these hills. There is however, no river through this valley, and the only river we encounter on the journey we are about to take is the Wandle. This rises near Croydon, then flows west nearly to Carshalton, then north to Mitcham, then north-westwards parallel to and just south of our railway through open parkland to Morden. The Wandle then continues northwards through Merton and Earlsfield to join the Thames at Wandsworth. It powered about 40 water mills mostly in its lower reaches more than 200 years ago, making this a very early and heavily industrialised area, whilst in its upper reaches there were several large watercress beds.

The centre of the town of Wimbledon rises to just above the 100-foot contour line, but this soon falls gradually to be about 50 from near Morden to Mitcham Junction, then slowly climbs to about 150 in the centre of Croydon and 180 feet at Addiscombe, falling again slowly to about 100 feet above sea level in Beckenham. The whole of our route from Wimbledon through Croydon to just before Elmers End and just before Birkbeck was in the County of Surrey until 1964, but the final two miles into Beckenham were in Kent. All are now in Greater London. The part of our route through the Wandle Valley is mainly on gravel, but as we approach Croydon we encounter chalk, and then London clay in the Woodside area, and it is again mostly gravel as we pass through Addiscombe to Beckenham.

Both Beddington and Croydon are of great antiquity, dating back to Anglo-Saxon times. Croydon became a Borough in 1883, and a County Borough in 1889, a great honour, for there were only two other County Boroughs in or anywhere near the London area. The name of the Woodside area arises from an ancient chain of oak forests around here. Much of the land to the west of Croydon formerly grew corn, but to the east the fields were mostly pasture. Today almost all agriculture has vanished, after 150 years of building more and more houses, also various light industries such as clockmaking, filming, lemonade, cement, bricks, etc. although there are still plenty of open spaces and parkland. Just before we reach our terminus at Beckenham we cross a little stream called The Beck, which flows into the Pool River, but it is not significant enough to make a valley.

HISTORICAL BACKGROUND

The new Croydon Tramlink, which opened in the Summer of 2000 after nearly a year of test running and driver training, is largely on the site of two full-size railways which were abandoned on Saturday evening 31 May 1997, and alongside a shorter section of railway which still remains open. This present volume is mainly a study of these railways as they were in May 1997. Tramlink has three basic routes, and about one third of the total is on new ground which was not previously railway, and is on, or alongisde, or near to public highways. The three basic routes are from the centre of Croydon to Wimbledon, to Beckenham with a branch to Elmers End, and to New Addington. The last mentioned has only ¾ mile of railway origin, and is omitted from our journey from Wimbledon to Beckenham, but these two termini are both at very important and busy main-line railway stations.

The total system is about 17¾ miles long. Of this, 7½ miles revives railways closed in May 1997, 1¾ miles is on the site of a railway closed in 1983, 1¾ miles is alongside a railway that is still active, 4½ miles are alongside public roads or across open country, and 2¼ miles are on public streets. Only this last 2¼, all in the very centre of Croydon, is the traditional street tramway of the type formerly so common in every large town in

Britain, and the entire system is operated by Continental-style two-section articulated single-deck tramcars, very different from the normal British double-decker. Croydon is only the fourth British example, after Manchester, Sheffield, and Wolverhampton, of the modern idea of operating former heavy railways with lightweight tramcars and extending them from the railway terminus right into the centre of the town along public streets.

The Tramlink route from Wimbledon to West Croydon, 6¼ miles, is entirely on the railway closed in 1997, except for small local diversions at Mitcham Junction and approaching West Croydon terminus. From Wimbledon, at a junction with the main line of the London & South Western Railway, the railway as far as Merton Park Station, ¾ mile, was opened on 22 October 1855 and owned jointly by the London & South Western Railway and the London Brighton & South Coast Railway. All the rest of the route, 5½ miles, to a junction with an existing LBSCR line at West Croydon, was opened on the same day, but wholly owned after the first eleven years by the LBSCR. Of the stations, only Mitcham and Beddington Lane were opened with the line. Morden Road followed in 1857, Mitcham Junction on 1 October 1868, Merton Park on 1 November 1870 and Waddon Marsh not until 6 July 1930. The entire route was electrified on 6 July 1930 on the third-rail system. From just west of Mitcham Station to just east of Waddon Marsh Halt the route followed the course of the early pioneer Surrey Iron Railway, which ran from Wandsworth to Croydon (and later to Merstham), and was in use from 26 July 1803 until 31 August 1846.

West Croydon Station has always been in one part of the central business area of Croydon town, and with the railway from Wimbledon running direct to here, the chief advantage Tramlink gives to passengers from Wimbledon, apart from an enormous increase in the frequency of service (every 10 minutes instead of 45), is the extension on the streets through to the far side of the town and beyond, but all at the sacrifice of much less comfortable seating. On the other hand the predecessors of the Tramlink routes to Elmers End and Beckenham have never had a railway route direct to the town centre. The

terminal station called Addiscombe was one mile away from West Croydon Station and most of the town centre, and for many years had been suffering from being nowhere in particular, obviously needing an extension, which was totally impossible in a heavily built-up residential area. East Croydon station, an extremely important point on the main London to Brighton railway, is roughly half-way between West Croydon and Addiscombe stations, but plays no part in the Tramlink story except for the road outside it now being an important part of the Tramlink street route connecting the Wimbledon and Beckenham railways.

The railway from Addiscombe station to Elmers End, 1¾ miles (and onwards to join a line from Charing Cross) was opened on 1 April 1864 by the Mid-Kent Railway Company, which was taken over in 1866 by the South Eastern Railway Company. A station was added at Woodside in 1871, and the route was electrified on 28 February 1926. For Tramlink, only the section from Woodside Junction to Elmers End station is being used, and Addiscombe to Woodside, ¾ mile, is permanently abandoned, although a preservation society was trying to take it over.

From Woodside station a railway to Selsdon was opened on 10 August 1885 jointly by the South Eastern and the LBSCR, with a station at Coombe Road. Bingham Road station was added on 1 September 1906. This route was electrified on 30 September 1935, but closed and totally abandoned on 13 May 1983. From Woodside, the first mile as far as a point now given the name of Sandilands has now been reopened for the Elmers End and Beckenham Tramlink routes, and the ¾ mile from Sandilands as far as Coombe Road, now renamed as Lloyd Park, has been reopened for the New Addington route, but the original through route is thus broken.

The Elmers End and Beckenham Tramlink routes are linked to the Wimbledon line by new street tramways through the town centre. There is a loop connecting West Croydon and East Croydon stations by two different routes and then along Addiscombe Road to Sandilands. At a point nearly halfway from Woodside station to Elmers End station, close to Macclesfield Road and now given the name of Arena, a new Tramlink branch with no railway or road origin strikes off to the left and runs around the edge of the former Croydon Corporation refuse destructor and the former sewage farm, and then the edge of the Crystal Palace District Cemetery.

It meets the still existing former London Chatham & Dover Railway branch from Crystal Palace, which was opened on 3 May 1858 and electrified on 3 March 1929, and runs for 1¾ miles along the south side of this to join the main line of the LCDR at Penge Junction and continue to Beckenham Junction Station. The Crystal Palace to Beckenham service runs only every half hour and, although originally double track, this end of it was singled some years ago, thus leaving a vacant space which Tramlink has now occupied, with two independent parallel single tracks instead of one double track. A station was added on this railway at Birkbeck on 2 March 1930, and Tramlink now has two additional stops between here and Beckenham, as well as Birkbeck.

Timetable from May 1990 to May 1997.

Wimbledon — Mitcham and West Croydon.

Mondays to Fridays

Miles		1	1	1		1	1	1		1	1	1		1	1	1		1	1	1		1	1	1		
0	**Wimbledon** ⊖ 152, 179 d	06 37	07 21	08 07	.....	08 53	09 37	10 21	.....	11 06	11 51	12 37	.....	13 21	14 06	14 51	.....	15 37	16 21	17 06	.....	17 53	18 38	19 21	.....	.....
0½	Merton Park d	06 39	07 23	08 09	.	08 55	09 39	10 23	.	11 08	11 53	12 39	.	13 23	14 08	14 53	.	15 39	16 23	17 08	.	17 55	18 40	19 23	.	.
1¼	Morden Road d	06 40	07 24	08 10	.....	08 56	09 40	10 24	.....	11 09	11 54	12 40	.....	13 24	14 09	14 54	.....	15 40	16 24	17 09	.....	17 56	18 41	19 24	.....	.....
2¼	Mitcham d	06 43	07 27	08 13	.	08 59	09 43	10 27	.	11 12	11 57	12 43	.	13 27	14 12	14 57	.	15 43	16 27	17 12	.	17 59	18 44	19 27	.	.
3	Mitcham Junction 179 d	06 46	07 30	08 16	.....	09 02	09 46	10 30	.....	11 15	12 00	12 46	.....	13 30	14 15	15 00	.....	15 46	16 30	17 15	.....	18 02	18 47	19 30	.....	.....
3¾	Beddington Lane d	06 48	07 32	08 18	.	09 04	09 48	10 32	.	11 17	12 02	12 48	.	13 32	14 17	15 02	.	15 48	16 32	17 17	.	18 04	18 49	19 32	.	.
5	Waddon Marsh d	06 51	07 35	08 21	.....	09 07	09 51	10 35	.....	11 20	12 05	12 51	.....	13 35	14 20	15 05	.....	15 51	16 35	17 20	.....	18 07	18 52	19 35	.....	.....
6¼	**West Croydon** 178 a	06 55	07 39	08 25	.	09 11	09 55	10 39	.	11 24	12 09	12 55	.	13 39	14 24	15 09	.	15 55	16 39	17 24	.	18 11	18 56	19 39	.	.

Saturdays

	1	1		1	1		1	1		1	1		1	1		1	1		1	1		1	1		1	
Wimbledon ⊖ 152, 179 d	06 37	07 21	.....	08 07	08 53	.....	09 37	10 21	.....	11 06	11 51	.....	12 37	13 21	.....	14 06	14 51	.....	15 37	16 21	.....	17 06	17 53	.....	18 38	.....
Merton Park d	06 39	07 23	.	08 09	08 55	.	09 39	10 23	.	11 08	11 53	.	12 39	13 23	.	14 08	14 53	.	15 39	16 23	.	17 08	17 55	.	18 40	.
Morden Road d	06 40	07 24	.....	08 10	08 56	.....	09 40	10 24	.....	11 09	11 54	.....	12 40	13 24	.....	14 09	14 54	.....	15 40	16 24	.....	17 09	17 56	.....	18 41	.....
Mitcham d	06 43	07 27	.	08 13	08 59	.	09 43	10 27	.	11 12	11 57	.	12 43	13 27	.	14 12	14 57	.	15 43	16 27	.	17 12	17 59	.	18 44	.
Mitcham Junction 179 d	06 46	07 30	.....	08 16	09 02	.....	09 46	10 30	.....	11 15	12 00	.....	12 46	13 30	.....	14 15	15 00	.....	15 46	16 30	.....	17 15	18 02	.....	18 47	.....
Beddington Lane d	06 48	07 32	.	08 18	09 04	.	09 48	10 32	.	11 17	12 02	.	12 48	13 32	.	14 17	15 02	.	15 48	16 32	.	17 17	18 04	.	18 49	.
Waddon Marsh d	06 51	07 35	.....	08 21	09 07	.....	09 51	10 35	.....	11 20	12 05	.....	12 51	13 35	.....	14 20	15 05	.....	15 51	16 35	.....	17 20	18 07	.....	18 52	.....
West Croydon 178 a	06 55	07 39	.	08 25	09 11	.	09 55	10 39	.	11 24	12 09	.	12 55	13 39	.	14 24	15 09	.	15 55	16 39	.	17 24	18 11	.	18 56	.

Mondays to Fridays

	1	1	1		1	1	1		1	1	1		1	1	1		1	1	1		1	1	1			
West Croydon 178 d	06 15	06 59	07 45	.....	08 30	09 15	09 59	.....	10 43	11 28	12 15	.....	12 59	13 43	14 28	.....	15 15	15 59	16 43	.....	17 28	18 15	18 59	.....	.....	.....
Waddon Marsh d	06 18	07 02	07 48	.	08 33	09 18	10 02	.	10 46	11 31	12 18	.	13 02	13 46	14 31	.	15 18	16 02	16 46	.	17 31	18 18	19 02	.	.	.
Beddington Lane d	06 21	07 05	07 51	.....	08 36	09 21	10 05	.....	10 49	11 34	12 21	.....	13 05	13 49	14 34	.....	15 21	16 05	16 49	.....	17 34	18 21	19 05	.....	.....	.....
Mitcham Junction 179 d	06 23	07 07	07 54	.	08 38	09 24	10 07	.	10 51	11 36	12 24	.	13 07	13 51	14 36	.	15 24	16 07	16 51	.	17 36	18 24	19 07	.	.	.
Mitcham d	06 25	07 09	07 56	.....	08 40	09 26	10 09	.....	10 53	11 38	12 26	.....	13 09	13 53	14 38	.....	15 26	16 09	16 53	.....	17 38	18 26	19 09	.....	.....	.....
Morden Road d	06 28	07 12	07 59	.	08 43	09 29	10 12	.	10 56	11 41	12 29	.	13 12	13 56	14 41	.	15 29	16 12	16 56	.	17 41	18 29	19 12	.	.	.
Merton Park d	06 29	07 13	08 00	.....	08 44	09 30	10 13	.....	10 57	11 42	12 30	.....	13 13	13 57	14 42	.....	15 30	16 13	16 57	.....	17 42	18 30	19 13	.....	.....	.....
Wimbledon ⊖ 152, 179 a	06 32	07 16	08 03	.	08 48	09 33	10 16	.	11 00	11 45	12 33	.	13 16	14 00	14 45	.	15 33	16 16	17 00	.	17 46	18 33	19 17	.	.	.

Saturdays

	1	1		1	1		1	1		1	1		1	1		1	1		1	1		1	1			
West Croydon 178 d	06 59	07 45	.....	08 30	09 15	.....	09 59	10 43	.....	11 28	12 15	.....	12 59	13 43	.....	14 28	15 15	.....	15 59	16 43	.....	17 28	18 15	.....	.....	.....
Waddon Marsh d	07 02	07 48	.	08 33	09 18	.	10 02	10 46	.	11 31	12 18	.	13 02	13 46	.	14 31	15 18	.	16 02	16 46	.	17 31	18 18	.	.	.
Beddington Lane d	07 05	07 51	.....	08 36	09 21	.....	10 05	10 49	.....	11 34	12 21	.....	13 05	13 49	.....	14 34	15 21	.....	16 05	16 49	.....	17 34	18 21	.....	.....	.....
Mitcham Junction 179 d	07 07	07 54	.	08 38	09 24	.	10 07	10 51	.	11 36	12 24	.	13 07	13 51	.	14 36	15 24	.	16 07	16 51	.	17 36	18 24	.	.	.
Mitcham d	07 09	07 56	.....	08 40	09 26	.....	10 09	10 53	.....	11 38	12 26	.....	13 09	13 53	.....	14 38	15 26	.....	16 09	16 53	.....	17 38	18 26	.....	.....	.....
Morden Road d	07 12	07 59	.	08 43	09 29	.	10 12	10 56	.	11 41	12 29	.	13 12	13 56	.	14 41	15 29	.	16 12	16 56	.	17 41	18 29	.	.	.
Merton Park d	07 13	08 00	.....	08 44	09 30	.....	10 13	10 57	.....	11 42	12 30	.....	13 13	13 57	.....	14 42	15 30	.....	16 13	16 57	.....	17 42	18 30	.....	.....	.....
Wimbledon ⊖ 152, 179 a	07 16	08 03	.	08 48	09 33	.	10 16	11 00	.	11 45	12 33	.	13 16	14 00	.	14 45	15 33	.	16 16	17 00	.	17 46	18 33	.	.	.

No Sunday Service

PASSENGER SERVICES

Wimbledon to West Croydon

The train service in 1855 was only six per day, and two on Sundays. This gradually increased to 10 or 12 by 1910, with five on Sundays, and then to 16 per day with eight on Sundays by 1914. In steam days a few journeys continued beyond Croydon to Crystal Palace. In 1930 with electrification the service became half-hourly on weekdays and hourly on Sundays. During the 1939-45 war, the weekday service also became only hourly. Later, for a few years it was every 20 minutes, which needed two trains to work it, but with not really enough terminal or recovery time. Then until May 1990 the service was back again to only half-hourly, with a journey time of 16 or 17 minutes, and 13 minutes standing time at Wimbledon and 14 at West Croydon. The two trains crossed each other at Mitcham Junction, where for a short distance there were two tracks. Finally from May 1990 until May 1997 the service was worked with only one train, running every 45 minutes, except that on the final day only, there was a two-train half-hourly service. After electrification the route was worked with the 1801-12 series (usually 1809-12) of ex-LBSCR two-car units from the South London line, and then later by the 2EPB type, and finally from October 1991 by two-car Class 456 units. Today the same journey takes 21 minutes, but with seven extra stops.

Addiscombe to Elmers End

Until the turn of the century there were usually about 20 trains on weekdays, but only four on Sundays, mostly running through to Charing Cross. By 1911 there were 34 trains on weekdays with 13 on Sundays, by 1924 these were 38 and 15, and by 1936 this had grown to

59 and 32. From 26 September 1949 the Addiscombe branch was reduced to a short shuttle service, to and from Elmers End only. From 13 September 1958 this became only hourly, but was back again to three per hour by the following November. It then became half-hourly from 11 June 1963, three per hour from 3 May 1976, and back to half hourly from 14 May 1984, connecting nicely at Elmers End with the half-hourly Charing Cross trains from Hayes. But this half-hourly shuttle must have been very uneconomic, because the running time was only five minutes each way, with four minutes standing time at Elmers End and 16 at Addiscombe. Latterly the service was worked with the new Class 466 two-car units.

Woodside to Coombe Road (and Selsdon)

This also was only a shuttle service from and to Elmers End for most of its short life, with a few trains from Charing Cross in the early days. Not opening until 1885 it had nine trains each weekday by 1890, 20 by 1911, nothing from 1917 until 1935, and 33 by 1936. Latterly, up until abandonment in 1983, the service was at rush hours only, seven trains in the morning and ten in the evening.

Birkbeck to Beckenham

The initial service of four trains had been increased to 12 by the time it was withdrawn in 1915. When replaced by electric trains in 1929, there were three trains per hour from and to Victoria via Streatham Hill and Crystal Palace until 1939.

A regular half-hourly service has been maintained subsequently, although there were cut backs in some years.

WIMBLEDON TO MORDEN ROAD

1.   Ex-LBSCR unit no. 1811 approaches Wimbledon Station from the London end on 18 November 1949. The Wimbledon to West Croydon service always ran under the route number of "2" in a series running from 1 to 99. (National Railway Museum)

Other views of Wimbledon are contained in:
Kingston & Wimbledon Tramways
Lines around Wimbledon
Mitcham Junction Lines
Waterloo to Woking

2.   Wimbledon station has ten platforms, nos 1-4 for the District Line, 5-8 for the Waterloo main lines, and 9-10 for services to (left) and from (right) Sutton or West Croydon. The West Croydon Tramlink service now terminates at the far end of platform 10, and the Sutton service from and to London now uses no. 9 in both directions.

3.   Soon after leaving Wimbledon, we come to Dundonald Road level crossing. Here we are looking back towards Wimbledon, only a few days after closure, when this wire barrier had already been erected across the tracks. There were formerly two sidings on the left side of this picture.

4.   At the same level crossing Dundonald Road is behind us, and we are looking to the north into Hartfield Crescent, while no. 456013 has had the first minute or two of its journey to West Croydon.

→

5.   In the days when this crossing still had ordinary gates and not lifting barriers, they were controlled by this signal box, which closed in 1983. Here on 20 April 1958 we are looking to the south, with Dundonald Road on the right. (A.E.Bennett)

3rd . SINGLE

Merton Park to

WIMBLEDON

1d.   FARE   1d.

FOR CONDITIONS SEE OVER.

4458   4458

→

6.   In this view of the same crossing we are looking along Dundonald Road, from Hartfield Crescent, with the railway to Wimbledon on the right.

7.   About 600 yards further along the railway there was another level crossing, at Kingston Road, visible at the bottom of this picture. We are looking back towards Wimbledon, with Hartfield Road on the right.

8.   Here we are looking along Kingston Road to the east during the 1930s. Hartfield Road and the railway to Wimbledon are on the left, a signal box long since demolished is in the centre, and Merton Park station is a short distance to the right. (Commercial postcard)

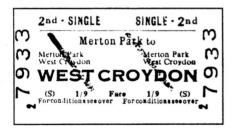

9.   This view of Kingston Road and its level crossing is the same as picture no. 8, but taken just about sixty years later.

10. As we stand on Kingston Road level crossing looking to the south east in 1997, we can just see Merton Park platform in the distance. Although soon to be abandoned, the track at the bottom of the picture has recently been relaid with flat bottom rails, concrete sleepers, and Pandrol rail fastenings to main line standards.

11. We are now about half-way from Kingston Road level crossing to Merton Park Station. This was formerly a junction, but it is now 1975 and the rails of the former double track to Merton Abbey and Tooting on the left have been removed, leaving only the single track of our route to West Croydon on the right. (H.F.Wheeller)

12. We are standing on the end of the platform at Merton Park Station while no. 456013 approaches Kingston Road level crossing on its journey to Wimbledon. This is double track all the way, but from here to West Croydon it is now almost entirely single track. The site of the Merton Abbey line and its junction are on the right.

13.   This view of Merton Park station looking towards the junction shows that in the old days the railway from Merton Abbey and Tooting was regarded as more important, with two tracks, two waiting shelters, and substantial buildings, while the West Croydon line on the extreme left had almost nothing. Here on 3 March 1962, 33 years after the pasenger service ceased, the station name is still displayed on the Tooting platform. (J.N.Faulkner)

14.   The quite substantial station buildings at Merton Park, had by 1997 lost all their former glory and acquired one of the biggest displays of amateur graffiti to be seen anywhere along this railway.

15.   Looking away from the junction at Merton Park station along the railway towards Merton Abbey and beyond, on 2 March 1929, we see a motor train approaching with engine no. E 243. This railway was owned jointly by the LSWR and the LBSCR, opened on 1 October 1868, lost its passenger service on 3 March 1929, and was closed to goods and abandoned on 1 May 1972. (H.C.Casserley)

16.   The very long footbridge visible in photo no. 15, spanning both the Tooting and the Croydon lines and a lot of ground in between, had by 1997 been drastically shortened so as to span only the Croydon line, and even this has been demolished for Tramlink.

18.   By 1997 Morden Road Halt had only this little corrugated iron shelter, which no. 456013 visited in both directions. There never was a second track or platform here, so far as is known.

←———

17.   The next station is Morden Road Halt. Here on 17 April 1955 we are looking back from the road bridge towards Wimbledon. All the platform buildings visible here were demolished 27 years later. (N.L.Browne)

19.   Looking the other way on 14 May 1961 we again see the substantial building which was later demolished. The bridge carries Morden Road itself, and has sufficient space for the track to be doubled. (Pamlin Prints)

20.   Morden Road Halt had more green trees than anything else by 1997. The exit on Morden Road itself at the top of the steps was extremely small and inconspicuous, with only the very smallest of nameboards and no building or hut.

PHIPPS BRIDGE TO MITCHAM

21.   About 400 yards beyond Morden Road was this footbridge, leading from Morden Hall Park on the south side of the railway, to a footpath in the foreground which led to Phipps Bridge a quarter mile away. Deer Park Road, famous for processing many amateur photographs and slides, is just off to the right.

22.   Standing on the footbridge shown in picture 21, we see in the foreground the bridge over one branch of the River Wandle, and in the far distance the bridge over the other branch. These two unite at Phipps Bridge, a quarter mile away to the left, and no. 456013 is in effect on an island.

23.   This is another view of the bridge seen in No. 22. With the very large Morden Hall Park on the right, the area is very rural, although there is a housing estate only a short distance beyond the trees at the top of the picture.

———————▶

24.   Here is the south side of the second of the two bridges over the two halves of the River Wandle mentioned in caption 22. There is a lovely old water mill, still in good working order, only 100 yards or so away.

25.   Another quarter mile along the railway brings us to another footbridge, seen here, which is at the end of Phipps Bridge Road, a cul-de-sac, and about 700 yards from Phipps Bridge itself. Tramlink has a new stop, not previously a station on the railway, halfway between the bridges in pictures 24 and 25, and this is called Phipps Bridge.

———————▶

26.   Here is the south side, in Morden Hall Park, of the footbridge whose north side we saw in picture no. 25. Like most other footbridges on Tramlink, this one has now been demolished, and whereas pedestrians were formerly protected from a train every 45 minutes, they now have to cross on the level and face the hazard of a tram every ten minutes, though admittedly easier for perambulators and wheelchairs.

27.   From the footbridge in photos 25 and 26 a further quarter mile brings us to this one at Ravensbury Path, whose north side we see here. There is another extra stop here for Tramlink, with the name of Belgrave Walk.

⟶

28.   Standing on Ravensbury Path footbridge on 23 June 1957 and looking towards Mitcham, we see 2EPB unit no. 5763, with a goods only track on the left. Hidden amongst the trees and bushes in the distance, hence difficult to photograph, was yet another footbridge, at Barons Walk, and at about the same spot the former Surrey Iron Railway trailed in from the left. (F.Hornby)

29.   Very soon after Barons Walk we come to Mitcham Station, on the east side of London Road, an important highway from London to Reigate. The station entrance was formerly through the very small arch in this large building, with the brick parapet of the bridge over the railway on the right, seen on 14 May 1961. (Pamlin Prints)

30.　　More recently this large building was closed, though it does still exist, and the entrance to Mitcham Station was transferred to this hole in the wall of the parapet, from where passengers had to walk along to the right behind the wall on a footbridge close to it, with steps down to the platform on the right of the picture.

31.　　From the top of the steps in picture no. 30, on the extreme right here, we look down eastwards onto the platform of Mitcham Station. There was formerly a second track and platform on the left, making a useful passing loop.

32.　　Mitcham signal box, with two semaphore signals at a very low level alongside it, and seen here on 13 August 1950, was closed in 1982. It stood where the bottom of the steps mentioned in 30 and 31 are now, and in the top right we can just see London Road bridge. (Pamlin Prints)

33.   We are looking to the west at Mitcham Station, after the signal box had been demolished. The new footbridge mentioned in picture no. 30 as being close to the main London Road bridge can be seen here. It replaced a previous footbridge of more coventional design which formerly stood somewhat closer to the camera in the days when there was a second track and platform on the right.

——————▶

34.   Locomotive no. B 615 heads a Wimbledon to West Croydon train on 26 March 1929, some 14½ months before electrification. The two traditional platform canopies have long since vanished, the one on the right totally, and the one on the left replaced by a rough and ready iron shelter with a small brick building adjacent. (H.C.Casserley)

——————▶

35.   Mitcham Station in its heyday had two extremely long platforms, long enough for a full length train, but for most of its life trains were never more than two coaches long. Here we are looking west from near the east end. The Tramlink station is now in the foreground of this view.

36.   Mitcham Station was on the site of the original 1803 Surrey Iron Railway, and so the parallel road alongside it was named Tramway Path, a name which it still has to this day. A little way beyond the east end of the station Tramway Path bends to the north and crosses the railway by this bridge, which has been demolished so that pedestrians now have to cross on the level.

⟶

37.   Standing on Tramway Path bridge and looking to the east we see where the single track through Mitcham Station becomes double in readiness for Mitcham Junction half a mile beyond. Until blocked by a landslide in 1971, this double track had started on the west side of the London Road bridge.

MITCHAM JUNCTION TO BEDDINGTON LANE

38.   Shortly before reaching Mitcham Junction, we pass under Willow Lane bridge. Nearly 200 years ago the Hackbridge branch of the Surrey Iron Railway turned off to the right just beyond the bridge.

39.   From the west end of Mitcham Junction station we look back to Willow Lane bridge, visible in the far distance. On the right is the ex-LBSCR line from Streatham, opened on 1 October 1868 and electrified on 3 March 1929. As the Wimbledon line was there first the Streatham line had to make a very sharp curve to join it. Until 1928 there was a signal box in the angle between the two routes.

40.   We look east from the west end of Mitcham Junction station, with the main buildings on the left. Although a relative newcomer, over the years the Streatham to Sutton line became far more important than our Wimbledon to West Croydon route.

41.   This view of Mitcham Junction Station is looking from west to east. By far the most important intermediate station on the Wimbledon to West Croydon line, this was also the halfway point, hence when a two train service was running, this was the place where they passed each other.

42.   Standing on the footbridge of Mitcham Junction station on 20 June 1991 we see 2EPB unit no. 6321 on its way to Wimbledon. In the distance the main line to Sutton forks to the right, whilst the West Croydon line straight ahead immediately returns to single track. (J.Scrace)

43.   From near the east end of Mitcham Junction station on 13 October 1962 we look back towards the footbridge, with Carshalton Road bridge beyond it and the station buildings on the right. These have not altered much over the years, although no longer used for railway purposes. (J.N.Faulkner)

44.   The westbound platform at Mitcham Junction was a lot longer than the eastbound one, as seen here. The new Tramlink completely bypasses this station by having new platforms of its own in former woodland paralleling it on the left.

45.   At the east end of Mitcham Junction station in 1930, we see a Stroudley two-coach railmotor steam push-pull train coming off the single track from West Croydon and handing in the staff at the signal box. The route to Sutton is on the right, opened on 1 October 1868 and electrified on 3 March 1929. (H.F.Wheeller)

46.   Looking east, we see the route to Sutton on the right, the start of the single track line to West Croydon in the centre, the footbridge between the two halves of the golf course in the distance, and on the left the signal box which was closed in 1982 but was still standing in 1997, derelict and with the inevitable display of graffiti. The new Tramlink bypasses the tracks seen here, has a new bridge to pass over the Sutton railway and rejoins the West Croydon railway shortly beyond.

47.   Standing on the golf club footbridge, we look backwards and see the station, the junction, the line to Sutton on the left and an electrical sub-station on the right. This bridge has also been demolished.

48.   The golf course, together with the rest of Mitcham Common of which it is a part, stretches ¾ mile to Beddington Lane. Standing on its level crossing on 13 October 1962, we look back towards Mitcham and see Beddington Lane Halt and its signal box. (J.N.Faulkner)

49.   Beddington Lane (Halt until the 1960s) never had more more than the one platform, used in both directions. The signal box was closed in 1982 and later demolished, and a huge new industrial building, of which we here see only a small part, arrived in the 1990s. Unit no. 456003 stands at the platform.

50.   On 17 October 1954, when Beddington Lane Halt still had semaphore signals instead of colour lights, and the service was still worked by ex-LBSCR units in the 1801-12 series (No. 1810 on this day), we look towards West Croydon and note the two-car stop sign painted on the platform, which coincides with the end of the fence. Unlike most others, the platform here was only about three cars long. (D.Cullum)

51.   Beddington Lane still had its signal box, its semaphore signals, and its old style level crossing gates when this picture was taken on 30 July 1969. There has never been any bus service along the Lane itself, until a local firm started a minibus to Wallington in 1999, hence the nearby houses and small factories were wholly dependent on the railway. (J.Scrace)

52.   A view from the east end of Beddington Lane shows the level crossing and no. 456003. From immediately beyond the crossing there was formerly a separate goods line running alongside on the left for about 1½ miles, as far as Wandle Park, to serve various factories, cement works, gravel pits, a brewery, a fever hospital, depots, gasworks and power stations. For most of the way there was also a goods line on the right.

53.   Half a mile beyond Beddington Lane a road called Therapia Lane came as a dead end from the main Mitcham Road on the north side of the railway and continued as this footbridge, here seen from the south side. A new stop, not previously a station, has been made at Stonecroft Way, 100 yards to the right but named Therapia Lane, and the new rolling stock depot and headquarters of Tramlink have been built just off to the left of this picture on the site of a former cement works. The depot, with its approach sidings in the foreground of this picture and its eleven storage sidings beyond the far end, stretches from Stonecroft Way halfway back to Beddington Lane, and to give the site extra width the tramway has been slewed out north eastwards along all this length.

54. Most of the heavy industry between Beddington Lane and Wandle Park has been closed and its buildings demolished in recent years, leaving large areas of dereliction, but some large new enterprises have started up between Therapia Lane and Purley Way, enough to justify a new stop for Tramlink called Ampere Way. In this picture, standing on Purley Way bridge and looking towards Croydon, we see Waddon Marsh Halt and signal box as they were on 30 March 1980, the four tracks already reduced to only two. (F.Hornby)

55.   Earlier, we see Waddon Marsh Halt on 7 May 1969 in more of its former glory. In this picture, the electric power station, with its quite new cooling tower, was still in situ, and the gas holder still appeared to be nearly full. The goods lines on the outside were closed in 1976, and the signal box and signal gantry followed in 1982, but for the time being the two electric tracks and the island platform remained. The electric track and passing loop on the north side closed in 1984, and were removed, as also was the footbridge. (J.Scrace)

56.   Even earlier, back in 1955, we see the signal box, the island platform, and the footbridge from the opposite side of the railway. Passenger access to the footbridge was by a footpath on the extreme left from Gurney Crescent. The enormous gasworks building in the background, like almost everything else around here, was later demolished. (F.Hornby)

57.   By 1997 all that was left of Waddon Marsh station was just one platform, one track and a scruffy little hut. The train service carried far more passengers passing through than those boarding or alighting here. The skeleton of the gasholder remains, but it is empty. In the early 1800s the Surrey Iron Railway, whose route we have followed from Mitcham, forked off to the left a little beyond the end of this platform.

58.   As we now look back towards Wimbledon from Waddon Marsh Halt, no trace remains of the many buildings of the former enormous gasworks on both sides of the railway, nor the power station just off to the bottom right. In the distance is the bridge carrying Purley Way, and the two chimneys which are all that now survive of a second and much newer electric power station which formerly stood there.

59.   As we approach Croydon everything changes. We cross over the River Wandle again, and see tennis courts and the pleasant urban parkland of Wandle Park on the left, with residential houses on the right. We are standing on Vicarage Road footbridge, with the Park on the left and the Road on the right. Tramlink has another new stop here, called Wandle Park, where the railway never had one.

60.   The railway now goes round a long and sharp curve to the left, with a substantial change of direction from south eastwards to north eastwards. As we stand on St Johns Grove footbridge and look backwards, we see Wandle Park on the right and, on the left, the ex-LBSCR route from West Croydon to Sutton, which was opened on 10th May 1847.

61.   Here we see the footbridge from which the previous picture was taken, but looking in the opposite direction. St Johns Grove is on the right, where the sign is pointing, and Waddon New Road runs alongside the railway. This footbridge, like most others, has now been removed, but it has been replaced by a new one slightly further west. There is also a new bridge for Tramlink.

62.   From St. Johns Grove footbridge and looking towards West Croydon we see the single Wimbledon track on the left and the two tracks from and to Sutton on the right. There was no junction between the two railways here. From its new bridge over the two Sutton tracks the Tramlink descends to run alongside them on the right as far as just beyond Pitlake bridge, which we see in the distance.

63.   As we get nearer to Pitlake bridge we see a train on the Wimbledon line on the left and the space where Tramlink now is on the right. The two Sutton tracks in the centre were electrified with overhead AC wires on 1 April 1925 and converted to the third-rail DC system on 22 September 1929.

64.   From Pitlake bridge the Wimbledon railway continues alongside the two Sutton tracks to the London Road bridge and West Croydon Station, visible in the distance, but just behind the camera Tramlink now turns sharp right to start its street tramway section. It runs along Cairo New Road, and then sharp left along Tamworth Road, which had a conventional street tramway with double-deck cars from 1906 to 1935.

———————▶

65.   As we look towards Sutton from London Road bridge we see on the extreme left that Tamworth Road now rejoins Waddon New Road. The former had both old and new tram tracks laid in it. The Wimbledon track on the right is connected to the up line by a crossover just off the bottom right corner of the picture.

66.　　The passenger entrance to West Croydon Station has since 1928 been on London Road, the most important street through the town of Croydon, but until that time there were two separate entrances further along the platforms, one on each side.

67.　　The south-western end of West Croydon station has a substantial bridge which carries not only London Road but also the station entrance and booking office and several retail shops and flats. The track on the right is the Wimbledon line.

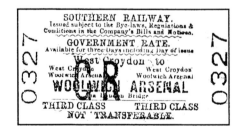

68.　　Looking back to this same bridge but from further away, we see ex-LBSCR former AC unit no. 1810 from Wimbledon terminating at the sand-drag. The two through tracks are from Sutton and beyond to Norwood and beyond. (Lens of Sutton)

69.   Here we have an end-on view of the terminus of the Wimbledon line, complete with modern friction buffers and 2EPB no. 6306, on 10 September 1987. The long slope for access to the platform on the left, instead of the usual stairway, is a feature more common on the LBSCR than elsewhere, although this one was of SR origin. (A.C.Mott)

70.   From the bottom of the steps at the passenger entrance to the up side of West Croydon station on 5 May 1970 we look along the Wimbledon platform and can just see its buffers in the distance. The main platform for trains to London, on the centre track here, does not start until beyond these buffers, giving passengers a very long walk from street to train. On the right 4 EPB unit no. 4381 is going to Sutton or beyond. (J.Scrace)

71.   The original entrance on the east side of West Croydon Station was closed in 1932 and now sells motorcar spares, and Tramlink now runs along Station Road in the foreground. There was no direct pre-1997 railway link from the Wimbledon railway to the Elmers End or Beckenham lines, so we must either walk one mile along Wellesley Road (north) and St James's Road or take bus 289 to Addiscombe Station, or else walk along Tramlink via Wellesley Road (south) and George Street to East Croydon Station or take bus 130, changing there to bus 312.

CENTRAL CROYDON AND ADDISCOMBE

72.   A tram of the South Metropolitan Electric Tramways & Lighting Co Ltd on the Crystal Palace route, which ran (this end of it) from 1902 to 1936, is seen here in Station Road, West Croydon, looking east from the London Road junction in about 1906-10. Rails for the new Tramlink have now been laid on exactly the same alignment. The large notice board on the pole on the left says "Cars start here for The Gloster, Norwood, Crystal Palace and Penge". Today's Tramlink stop is just a little further on, beyond the bend. All the buildings visible here are still exactly the same today, except only for the signwriting. (C.H.Price/J.B.Gent)

Other albums featuring Croydon:
Croydon's Trolleybuses
Croydon's Tramways (to 1951)
East Croydon to Three Bridges
London Bridge to East Croydon
Mitcham Junction Lines
Victoria to East Croydon
West Croydon to Epsom

73.	Wellesley Road, which runs parallel to the main London Road and North End but, 200 yards east of them, was a quiet backwater in 1910. Here we are looking north from George Street. For many years, and until much more recent times, all the north and south horse and electric tramways, also all the motor buses, used London Road, North End and High Street. (C.H.Price/J.B.Gent)

74.	Wellesley Road, again looking north from George Street crossroads, was drastically widened in the 1970s, and all trace of earlier buildings totally vanished. This is how it looked on 6 May 1995, with a short tunnel burrowing under George Street. Some of the Country buses were using Wellesley Road by 1939, but almost all of the numerous Central Area bus routes still used North End, the main shopping street, despite it being very narrow, until it was closed to all traffic in both directions in 1989, and everything was diverted via Wellesley Road. Today, Tramlink travels southbound along the right hand side of this picture, before turning left into George Street. (J.B.Gent)

75.　　The western half of George Street looked like this in the late 1980s. We are looking to the east from the bus stop outside no. 28 midway between North End and Wellesley Road. From 1901 to 1927 it was a part of the original Addiscombe tram route. Today Tramlink, in its clockwise tour of the centre of the town, travels westbound along here towards the camera, and has a stop outside the "Beauty" shop and "Allders" just off the left edge of the picture. All the buildings visible here are still exactly the same today. (J.B.Gent)

———————▶

76.　　Church Street, which is the continuation westwards of George Street, after descending the very steep Crown Hill, also now carries the westbound Tramlink tracks. Here in 1971 we are looking westwards from Frith Road, the turning on the right, but all the buildings are still the same 30 years later. Surprisingly Church Street has never had any bus services along it so far as I can trace, and all George Street services have always turned left or right into High Street or North End. (J.B.Gent)

———————▶

77.　　This is the eastern half of George Street, looking to the east from Wellesley Road on 6 May 1995. The 24 storey building in the centre distance, known as the NLA Tower (Noble Lowndes Associates), is just beyond East Croydon Railway station. Today the left hand side of the road seen here carries a double Tramlink track, one track coming from Wellesley Road at the bottom left and turning left, and the other going towards Church Street beyond the bottom centre. All other traffic is banished to the right hand side only of the road, or diverted elsewhere. (J.B.Gent)

78.   George Street had an electric tramway from 18 December 1901 to 31 March 1927, and again from 10 May 2000. We see two Croydon Corporation trams on the Addiscombe route passing East Croydon station on the main line of the LBSCR from Victoria to Brighton in about 1905. The station buildings seen here were totally demolished in the early 1990s and replaced by a weird looking steel utility structure, with the load suspended by cable from high girders. The road outside it is now the main mid-route terminus and timing point on Tramlink, with three tracks. (C.H.Price/J.B.Gent)

79.   Looking north from the roof of Essex House on 1 October 1961, we again see the exterior of East Croydon Station, with its six platforms beyond. There is no direct link between this railway and any of those involved in the Tramlink story except by long detours. (D.Cullum)

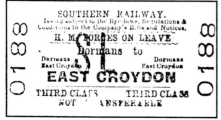

80.   If we walk from East Croydon Station or take bus 312 along Cherry Orchard Road and Lower Addiscombe Road we reach Addiscombe station, terminus until 31 May 1997 of the railway to Elmers End and beyond. This building, seen here on 19 October 1983 looking east, was opened in 1899 replacing the original 1864 structure.

81.   As we enter Addiscombe Station we come onto the end of the island platform, with its massive overhead canopy dating from 1896. The main all day service has always been worked to and from the right hand platform, with rush hour extras and slack hour berthing on the left, but there were two more tracks further to the right. This was the scene on 19 October 1983.

82.   At the outer end of Addiscombe station the island platform was shorter until 1957, and rail access to the left hand side was this side of the signal box instead of beyond it. Here is how it looked on 19 October 1983. Unfortunately the box was destroyed by fire by vandals just one year before closure, after which trains always ran with a pilotman in the cab.

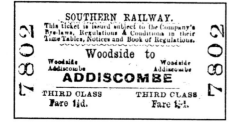

SOUTHERN RAILWAY.
This ticket is issued subject to the Company's Bye-laws, Regulations & Conditions in their Time Tables, Notices and Book of Regulations.

Woodside to

Woodside Addiscombe   Woodside Addiscombe

ADDISCOMBE

THIRD CLASS   THIRD CLASS
Fare 1½d.   Fare 1½d.

7802

83.   One of the shifts was worked regularly by a lady. Here we see Alice busy with her levers on 6 May 1995 after letting a Networker arrive. The route diagram above the levers still shows the junction with the Woodside and Selsdon line. (P. O'Callaghan).

84.　　On the day of closure of the Addiscombe railway, 31 May 1997, a group of people who were forming a preservation society had set up a stand in a corner of the station concourse to attract support from the public and to recruit members. A Carlton television crew also visited the stand and we see them filming for a showing on the daily "Your Shout" TV programme. The SECR Preservation Society are still hoping for success, but despite their title they don't expect to preserve the whole of the SECR, just this one station and the adjacent depot. (P. O'Callaghan)

85.　　A new four road carriage berthing depot was added in 1925 on the south eastern side of the railway just outside Addiscombe station. It was disused for several years before the railway closed, when Networker trains took over the service, and soon became overgrown with weeds and bushes, but the rails remained intact. Here we are looking east from the station platform.

> **Other views of this station and of Elmers End can be found in *London Bridge to Addiscombe*.**

86.　　Mid-way between Addiscombe station and Blackhorse Lane bridge this subway allowed local residents to cross under the railway. Known as Dalmally Passage, we see it looking north-west towards Morland Road.

BINGHAM ROAD TO WOODSIDE

87.   The railway from Addiscombe to Woodside, unlike the rest of the route to Elmers End, has not been incorporated into Tramlink. Instead, a new street tramway from East Croydon station has been made along Addiscombe Road as far as a point newly named Sandilands (from an adjacent road), where it joins the former Woodside to Selsdon railway abandoned on 13 May 1983. A quarter of a mile further on, it turns very sharply to the left to pass through Bingham Road station, seen here on 5 August 1980. (N.D.Mundy.)

88.   Bingham Road station was on an embankment, with the entrance just to the right of the advert posters which are seen here on 19 October 1983, where we are looking to the east along Bingham Road itself. The bridge was later removed, but the abutments remained until 1997, since when both they and the embankments on each side have been demolished down to ground level, to allow Tramlink to cross by a level crossing instead of a bridge.

89.   Here is the entrance to the up, or western, side of Bingham Road station as it was on 19 October 1983.

90.   The entrance to the down side of Bingham Road station, on the other side of the road bridge was separate from, but symmetrical with, picture no. 89. Both had a glass roof over the stairway leading up to the platforms, as seen here on 19 October 1983.

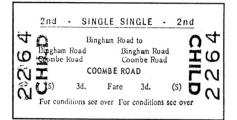

91.　　Only 100 yds north of Bingham Road, another bridge of exactly the same design took the railway over Lower Addiscombe Road, as seen looking to the east on 19 October 1983. Here also the bridge was removed fairly soon after abandonment but the abutments and embankment remained until 1997. The road here was an important main one, and still is, with two frequent trunk bus services (12 and 59A) to the centre of London. The bridge was high enough, though only just, to clear all types of double deck buses.

92.　　Looking to the south in 1997, we see the abutment of the former bridge over Lower Addiscombe Road, which has since been demolished down to ground level. The new Tramlink station has been established on the opposite side of Bingham Road and to occupy the space, at ground level, between there and this picture. It was advertised at first as still keeping the name of Bingham Road, but this was altered at the last moment to Addiscombe, nearly half a mile from the previous station of the same name.

93. On the north side of Lower Addiscombe Road, just to the right of The Candy Box, we see the other abutment of the former bridge. Whereas in the old days, with not so much road traffic, the road was protected from only two trains per hour each way by them being on the bridge, now that this road is exceptionally busy with a never ending stream of traffic, it has the major hazard of twelve Tramlink cars each way scheduled over this level crossing without even any gates. One fears that it will not be long before there is a major collision here, and probably several, as well as huge delays. It is difficult to understand why the embankment and two bridges have not been perpetuated.

→

94. Another quarter of a mile from the level crossing, the railway passes under Blackhorse Lane Bridge. Here we are looking from it on 19 October 1983, when it was still active, towards the junction with the railway to the (old) Addiscombe station. That line passed along this side of the houses visible on the left, and had its own separate bridge under Blackhorse Lane. Tramlink now has an extra new stop, not previously a station, in the bottom right corner of this picture, and with the name of Blackhorse Lane.

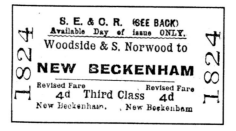

S. E. & C. R. (SEE BACK)
Available Day of issue ONLY.
Woodside & S. Norwood to
NEW BECKENHAM
Revised Fare   Revised Fare
4d Third Class 4d
New Beckenham.   , New Beckenham
2824   2824

95.   Next we come to Ashburton Park footbridge, on which we are standing in 1997 and looking back to the west along the Addiscombe line, whose bridge under Blackhorse Lane can be seen in the far distance. Until 1983 the railway to Bingham Road and Selsdon forked off to the left in the near foreground, by now lost in a jungle of trees and bushes.

96.   Now it is only a stone's throw to Woodside station, which had an extremely long platform. Standing on the very end of this and looking to the west we see Ashburton Park footbridge, built with a brick arch and probably originally intended as a road. The post, though not the signals above it, which formerly controlled the junction to the Selsdon line, could still dimly be seen on the left in 1997.

97.   From the western end of the long platform at Woodside station we look at the booking office. Formerly double track, only the right hand platform had been in use in recent years. There was formerly a large goods and coal yard on the left, with sidings, but this closed on 30 September 1963.

98.   Woodside station looking eastwards was recorded in November 1948 before both the platform canopies had been shortened, and before the grassy slope on the right had become covered with almost impenetrable bushes and small trees. (D.Clayton)

The route southwards from Woodside is featured in *Croydon to East Grinstead.*

99.   All the main station buildings at Woodside were on top of the bridge. Even in 1997 they still looked quite attractive, and back in their heyday they must have been very much so. Sadly in 1993 the windows were boarded up and the station became unstaffed.

100. The east elevation of Woodside station was on Spring Lane, a fairly important road and to some extent the continuation of Lower Addiscombe Road. The stairs down to the platform were formerly close to this end of the building, but moved latterly to be just off the left edge of the picture.

101. Here we are looking north east from Spring Lane bridge on 19 October 1983, with the houses in Estcourt Road on the left, but the view was still just about the same in 1997.

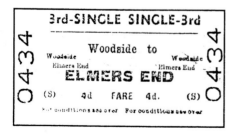

102. About one third of the way from Woodside station to Elmers End station was Macclesfield Road footbridge. Just beyond here a new stop, not previously a station, has been built for Tramlink, and is called Arena. About half way from Macclesfield Road to Elmers End a siding formerly trailed backwards on the north side of the line into Croydon Corporation's South Norwood refuse destructor. The sewage works was 400 yards further north.

ELMERS END

103.   The double track to Addiscombe is in the centre, the double track branching to Hayes is on the left, and the single track to the Addiscombe bay platform is on the right. The two pairs of through tracks were formerly much closer to the bay road, but were slewed out to the left in 1947, with a reverse curve back to the original straight course, so as to make space for the lengthening of the platforms to bring their ends much closer to the junction.

104.   The main through tracks to London are in the centre, while two-car Networker no. 466016 on the Addiscombe shuttle service is at the bay platform, on the last day, 31 May 1997.

105.   Standing on the same spot as the previous photo, we see that Elmers End station also formerly had, on the right hand side, a bay platform for the Hayes route, with an electrical sub station to the right of this.

106.   Networker unit no. 466016 stands at the bay platform in brilliant sunshine after arriving from Addiscombe, and is taking terminal layover before returning there. There was a coal depot to the left of the bay road until 1963.

107.   This photo is from 2 October 1954. The canopy roof on the left, and the entire canopy including its supporting posts on the right, were subsequently rebuilt to a different design. The middle part, on the right, is completely missing because of a 1941 air raid. (D.Cullum)

108.   Here we see the approach to the buffer stops on the bay road. The footbridge is much older, but all the buildings immediately beyond it were demolished in 1973 and replaced by simple utilitarian facilities.

109.   The traditional buffer stops of conventional design were augmented in recent years by a modern sliding friction buffer a little way in front of them, so as to stop the train in a controlled manner if it should hit it. No. 466016 has not hit it and is ready to return to Addiscombe.

Way out

110.   We are now standing on the footbridge looking away from London. An EPB standing at the Addiscombe bay platform, on the right, is almost hidden; the train from Hayes with which it connects is approaching, and the high building in the top left of the picture is the electrical sub station. (Lens of Sutton)

BIRKBECK TO BECKENHAM

111.   Just beyond the new Arena stop a completely new Tramlink branch goes off to the left, across open country behind the sites of the refuse destructor and sewage farm, then with another new Stop at Harrington Road, then around the edge of the cemetery, with a very sharp corner which brings it up alongside a still existing railway running from Crystal Palace to Beckenham Junction. About 300 yds later it passes through Birkbeck Station, seen on 2 October 1954, looking east. (D.Cullum)

112. The railway through Birkbeck was formerly double, but as it has only two trains per hour each way it was singled in 1983 as seen here, again looking to the east, thus leaving a space on the right for Tramlink to run alongside it for the next 1½ miles. The platform and separate entrance on the right were demolished, but have now been rebuilt on the same site for Tramlink.

113.   This railway is on a low embankment, and to pass under it Elmers End Road, with a new replacement bridge from modern times, has to dip down lower. Birkbeck station is on the extreme left of the picture.

114.   An unusual feature of Birkbeck station until 1997 was that the self service ticket issuing machine was at the bottom of the steps on the public highway in Elmers End Road, instead of up on the platform or in a separate building.

115.   Midway between Birkbeck station and Beckenham Road bridge, looking east, we come to Avenue Road with this footbridge. Another new stop, not previously a station, has been added here for Tramlink and named Avenue Road. This is the only footbridge on the route from Wimbledon to be retained and that is because it passes over the railway as well.

116.   Next the railway passes over Beckenham Road by this bridge, where we are looking to the north west. In the top right corner of this picture yet another new stop has been added for Tramlink. It is named Beckenham Road and has a passing loop, a little to the east.

117.   After another 200 yds this footpath, from Kings Hall Road to Thayers Farm Road, passes underneath the railway by this brick arch subway.

118.   The ex-LCDR route via Birkbeck joins the main line at Penge Junction, and runs alongside it for half a mile into Beckenham Junction station, where it terminates in the bay platform on the left of this picture.
(Lens of Sutton)

119.   Looking the opposite way towards the buffers we see a train from Victoria via Birkbeck at its terminus. Eurostar express trains now rush through from Waterloo to Paris and Brussels on the two tracks on the left, but Tramlink forks right as it approaches the station and terminates just outside, after branching into two tracks.

Other photographs of Beckenham are to be found in:
Charing Cross to Orpington
Clapham Junction to Beckenham Junction

120.   Tramlink now terminates in the forecourt of Beckenham Junction station just off the bottom left corner of this picture, and as we complete our pre-1997 journey from Wimbledon to Beckenham we really must admire these lovely ornamental cast iron brackets which support the canopy over the entrance to the south side of the station.

Middleton Press

Easebourne Lane, Midhurst, W Sussex. GU29 9AZ Tel: 01730 813169 Fax: 01730 812601
*If books are not available from your local transport stockist, order direct with cheque,
Visa or Mastercard, post free UK.*

BRANCH LINES
Branch Line to Allhallows
Branch Line to Alton
Branch Lines around Ascot
Branch Line to Ashburton
Branch Lines around Bodmin
Branch Line to Bude
Branch Lines around Canterbury
Branch Lines around Chard & Yeovil
Branch Lines around Cromer
Branch Lines to East Grinstead
Branch Lines of East London
Branch Lines to Effingham Junction
Branch Lines around Exmouth
Branch Line to Fairford
Branch Lines around Gosport
Branch Line to Hawkhurst
Branch Lines to Horsham
Branch Lines around Huntingdon
Branch Line to Ilfracombe
Branch Line to Kingswear
Branch Lines to Launceston & Princetown
Branch Lines to Longmoor
Branch Line to Looe
Branch Line to Lyme Regis
Branch Lines around March
Branch Lines around Midhurst
Branch Line to Minehead
Branch Line to Moretonhampstead
Branch Line to Padstow
Branch Lines around Plymouth
Branch Lines to Seaton and Sidmouth
Branch Line to Selsey
Branch Lines around Sheerness
Branch Line to Shrewsbury
Branch Line to Swanage *updated*
Branch Line to Tenterden
Branch Lines around Tiverton
Branch Lines to Torrington
Branch Lines to Tunbridge Wells
Branch Line to Upwell
Branch Lines of West London
Branch Lines around Weymouth
Branch Lines around Wisbech

NARROW GAUGE
Branch Line to Lynton
Branch Lines around Portmadoc 1923-46
Branch Lines around Porthmadog 1954-94
Branch Line to Southwold
Douglas to Port Erin
Kent Narrow Gauge
Two-Foot Gauge Survivors
Romneyrail
Southern France Narrow Gauge
Vivarais Narrow Gauge

SOUTH COAST RAILWAYS
Ashford to Dover
Bournemouth to Weymouth
Brighton to Eastbourne
Brighton to Worthing
Dover to Ramsgate
Eastbourne to Hastings
Hastings to Ashford
Portsmouth to Southampton
Southampton to Bournemouth

SOUTHERN MAIN LINES
Basingstoke to Salisbury
Bromley South to Rochester
Crawley to Littlehampton
Dartford to Sittingbourne
East Croydon to Three Bridges
Epsom to Horsham
Exeter to Barnstaple
Exeter to Tavistock
Faversham to Dover

London Bridge to East Croydon
Orpington to Tonbridge
Tonbridge to Hastings
Salisbury to Yeovil
Swanley to Ashford
Tavistock to Plymouth
Victoria to East Croydon
Waterloo to Windsor
Waterloo to Woking
Woking to Portsmouth
Woking to Southampton
Yeovil to Exeter

EASTERN MAIN LINES
Ely to Kings Lynn
Fenchurch Street to Barking
Ipswich to Saxmundham
Liverpool Street to Ilford

WESTERN MAIN LINES
Ealing to Slough
Exeter to Newton Abbot
Newton Abbot to Plymouth
Paddington to Ealing
Slough to Newbury

COUNTRY RAILWAY ROUTES
Andover to Southampton
Bath Green Park to Bristol
Bath to Evercreech Junction
Bournemouth to Evercreech Jn.
Cheltenham to Andover
Croydon to East Grinstead
Didcot to Winchester
East Kent Light Railway
Fareham to Salisbury
Frome to Bristol
Guildford to Redhill
Reading to Basingstoke
Reading to Guildford
Redhill to Ashford
Salisbury to Westbury
Stratford upon Avon to Cheltenham
Strood to Paddock Wood
Taunton to Barnstaple
Wenford Bridge to Fowey
Westbury to Bath
Woking to Alton
Yeovil to Dorchester

GREAT RAILWAY ERAS
Ashford from Steam to Eurostar
Clapham Junction 50 years of change
Festiniog in the Fifties
Festiniog in the Sixties
Isle of Wight Lines 50 years of change
Railways to Victory 1944-46
SECR Centenary album
Talyllyn 50 years of change
Yeovil 50 years of change

LONDON SUBURBAN RAILWAYS
Caterham and Tattenham Corner
Charing Cross to Dartford
Clapham Jn. to Beckenham Jn.
Crystal Palace (HL) & Catford Loop
East London Line
Finsbury Park to Alexandra Palace
Kingston and Hounslow Loops
Lewisham to Dartford
Lines around Wimbledon
London Bridge to Addiscombe
Mitcham Junction Lines
North London Line
South London Line
West Croydon to Epsom
West London Line
Willesden Junction to Richmond

London Suburban Railway continued .....
Wimbledon to Beckenham
Wimbledon to Epsom

STEAMING THROUGH
Steaming through Cornwall
Steaming through the Isle of Wight
Steaming through Kent
Steaming through West Hants
Steaming through West Sussex

TRAMWAY CLASSICS
Aldgate & Stepney Tramways
Barnet & Finchley Tramways
Bath Tramways
Bournemouth & Poole Tramways
Brighton's Tramways
Burton & Ashby Tramways
Camberwell & W.Norwood Tramways
Clapham & Streatham Tramways
Croydon's Tramways
Dover's Tramways
East Ham & West Ham Tramways
Edgware and Willesden Tramways
Eltham & Woolwich Tramways
Embankment & Waterloo Tramways
Enfield & Wood Green Tramways
Exeter & Taunton Tramways
Greenwich & Dartford Tramways
Hammersmith & Hounslow Tramways
Hampstead & Highgate Tramways
Hastings Tramways
Holborn & Finsbury Tramways
Ilford & Barking Tramways
Kingston & Wimbledon Tramways
Lewisham & Catford Tramways
Liverpool Tramways 1. Eastern Routes
Liverpool Tramways 2. Southern Routes
Liverpool Tramways 3. Northern Routes
Maidstone & Chatham Tramways
Margate to Ramsgate
North Kent Tramways
Norwich Tramways
Portsmouth's Tramways
Reading Tramways
Seaton & Eastbourne Tramways
Shepherds Bush & Uxbridge Tramway
Southampton Tramways
Southend-on-sea Tramways
Southwark & Deptford Tramways
Stamford Hill Tramways
Twickenham & Kingston Tramways
Victoria & Lambeth Tramways
Waltham Cross & Edmonton Tramway
Walthamstow & Leyton Tramways
Wandsworth & Battersea Tramways

TROLLEYBUS CLASSICS
Croydon Trolleybuses
Bournemouth Trolleybuses
Hastings Trolleybuses
Maidstone Trolleybuses
Reading Trolleybuses
Woolwich & Dartford Trolleybuses

WATERWAY ALBUMS
Kent and East Sussex Waterways
London to Portsmouth Waterway
West Sussex Waterways

MILITARY BOOKS
Battle over Portsmouth
Battle over Sussex 1940
Bombers over Sussex 1943-45
Bognor at War
Military Defence of West Sussex
Military Signals from the South Coast
Secret Sussex Resistance
Surrey Home Guard
Sussex Home Guard

OTHER RAILWAY BOOKS
Garraway Father & Son
Index to all Middleton Press stations
Industrial Railways of the South-East
South Eastern & Chatham Railways
London Chatham & Dover Railway
War on the Line (SR 1939-45)